Saxman
Native Village
otem Park
ALASKA

Cover image: A short raven entrance pole, at left, stands near a winged raven pole and the stairs to the Beaver Clan House used for ceremonial dancing in Saxman Native Village, three miles south of downtown Ketchikan.

Pages 2-3: A dozen totem poles and posts surround Totem Row in Saxman Totem Park as it joins Killer Whale Ave. where frog heads emerge from the wooden retaining walls in front of the Beaver Clan House.

Published by:
Todd Communications
611 E. 12th Ave., Suite 102
Anchorage, Alaska 99501-4603
Phone: 907-274-TODD (8633)
Fax: 907-929-5550
e-mail: sales@toddcom.com
WWW.ALASKABOOKSANDCALENDARS.COM

Photography: Cliff and Nancy Hollenbeck
Edited by: Irene Dundas and Frank Seludo
With editorial assistance by Dragon London and Nathan Jackson
Art Direction/Design: Vered R. Mares, **Todd Communications**

First printing April, 2013
ISBN: 978-1-57833-952-5

Printed by Everbest Printing Co., Ltd., in Guangzhou, China, through **Alaska Print Brokers**, Anchorage, Alaska.

Saxman
Native Village
Totem Park
ALASKA

Contents

Below: A cedar history of Saxman sign explains the origin of this concentration of Tlingit Indian totem poles.

SAXMAN

LEGEND : TLINGIT INDIAN VILLAGE, ESTABLISHED 1894, IS NAMED FOR SCHOOL TEACHER SAMUEL SAXMAN, ONE OF THREE MEN LOST DEC. OF 1886 WHILE SCOUTING FOR A NEW LOCATION FOR PEOPLE OF TONGASS AND CAPE FOX VILLAGES. TOTEMS HERE, COMPRISING WORLD'S LARGEST COLLECTION, INCLUDING POLES MOVED FROM PENNOCK, TONGASS, AND VILLAGE ISLANDS AND FROM OLD CAPE FOX VILLAGE AT KIRK POINT. MANY ARE POLES RESTORED UNDER FEDERAL WORKS PROJECT DIRECTED BY THE U.S. FOREST SERVICE BEGINNING IN 1939.

Right: Sun Raven Pole: The first pole completed for Saxman Totem Park, showing three adventures of Raven for this mortuary post. A sun halo around the head of raven with outspread wings is at the top. Three figures, the children of the sun, visited by Raven after the Deluge are between the wings. Diminutive faces within eyes adorn Raven's wings. These represent Raven's ability to change forms. The Sun Raven Totem is the clan property of the Taanta Kwaan, Ravens.

Totems

William Seward Shame Pole – This pole is topped by U.S. Secretary of State William H. Seward who negotiated the purchase of Alaska from Russia in 1867. He traveled to nearby Ft. Tongass on Tongass Island in 1869 and was honored with a potlatch and many gifts, including a cedar chest that he sits on here. His spruce root hat with banded top represents wealth. Tlingit Indians felt he should be shamed for failing to repay the hospitality of their Chief Ebbits.

Eagle atop the Beaver Pole on Totem Row

Giant Rock Oyster Memorial Pole – The external figure represented here is of a boy with his hand in the mouth of a giant oyster. The totem represents one of many clan stories from the Neix. Adi Eagle Clan House. The boy whose hand is caught in the giant oyster's mouth drowned when he could not pull it loose when trying to reach a devilfish. His descendants named themselves the Giant Rock Oyster House.

The Pointing Figure was originally on a short pole and made from the Taanta Kwaan for brothers of the Raven Bone House of the Raven Clan to mark their sister's grave, originally placed on nearby Pennock Island. The pointing figure, possibly a shaman, is wearing a wooden hat adorned with orcas, or killer whales, on the front. Originally carved about 1895, the detailed face and ears on this replacement pole indicate the carver may have been trying to depict a real person instead of a mythic character.

The Wolf House post shows the characteristic hanging tongue of a running wolf.

The Giant Rock Oyster Memorial is unique for its secondary off-the-pole carving

An Eagle atop a Beaver-based pole soars above the Dogfish Pole. The dogfish is like a small mud shark that lives on the ocean floor with halibut. They have saw-like teeth and have barbs on their top and tail fins.

The Sun Raven Pole against a cloudy Saxman sky.

Fine detail from the Raven Mistake Pole.

Fine adz or chisel marks show how the Wolf House Post was painstakingly carved by skilled totem carvers.

Four frogs from the Frog Wall – This decorated retaining wall illustrates the crest of the Kiks.
Adi frog Clan of the Saanya Kwaan People of Cape Fox/Saxman.

Left: A Beaver from the base of one of Saxman Village's Eagle Beaver Poles sits erect. Beaver totems often exhibit two distinct characteristics – large front teeth for cutting down trees and large cross-hatched black tails.

A Bear Entrance Pole in front of the Beaver Clan House where traditional ceremonies occur.

An Eagle Beaver Pole, left, and Owl Memorial Pole, right, frame a Raven Entrance Pole to the Beaver Clan House. The straight black beak is a characteristic of the raven at Saxman.

A Beaver at the based of an Eagle Beaver Pole at the intersection of Totem Row and Killer Whale Avenue.

Sea Bear Totem, a servant to the sea monster Gunakadeit of the Taanta Teikweidi.

A soaring eagle from an Eagle Beaver Pole. Southeast Alaska has a large population of bald eagles thanks in part to its abundance of fish – especially salmon.

The highly ornamental Loon Tree illustrates this freshwater bird that still lives in abundance on lakes throughout Alaska. The loon is depicted on this totem pole because it had aided clan members to safety.

The Giant Rock Oyster Pole illustrates four related houses of the Neix. Adi clan with the Eagle Claw House at the top. Claws on this human figure distinguish them from those of the Eagle clan. A beaver below the eagle represents the Beaver Dam House, atop a beaver representing the Beaver Tail House. The Giant Rock Oyster House is represented at the bottom of the pole.

Raven Entrance Pole - originally a house post from a clan of Taanta Kwaan - Tlingit people.

Audrey Daniels touches the teeth of the Giant Rock Oyster face.

Saxman People

Saanya Kwaan Cape Fox people of Saxman: Resplendent in button blankets and dance regalia, left to right: Clarita Seludo, Crista Seludo, Theophilus McBurnette, Teresa DeWitt, Lakrisha Hargrove, Tina Seludo, Jonathan Williams, Cody Boyd, Katrina Boyd, Isabella Boyd, Andrew Harris, Bill Williams, Maria Badgley, Tempa Major, Sherrie Potter, Jennifer Jackson, Joe Thomas.

Cape Fox dancer Teresa DeWitt in red cedar bark hat and button blanket cloak with totem-emblazoned drum.

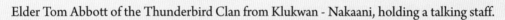

Elder Tom Abbott of the Thunderbird Clan from Klukwan - Nakaani, holding a talking staff.

Audrey Daniels is learning to dance in front of the Beaver House.

Back Row: Charlotte Davis, Alvina Martinez, Joe Thomas, Yvonne Watson, Kristy Evans, Tom Abbott.

Third Row: Maria Badgley, Geraldine Watson, Clarita Seludo, Isabella Boyd.

Second Row: Tamara Nunley, Dorian Dundas, Theophilus McBurnette, Robert Williams.

First Row: Jacob Williams, Kaylee Evans, Brandon Badgley, Marleina Dundas.

A portrait of a smiling Dorian Dundas

Young Saxman dancers Cody Boyd, Katrina Boyd, Isabella Boyd.

Richard Shields Jr. is ready to dance.

Dancer Forest DeWitt with carved wooden bear hat.

23

Double killer whales of the Tsaaqweidi Clan adorn the front of Joe Thomas' top and leggings.

Saxman Blankets

Back Row: Tempa Major, Raven Blanket. Clarita Seludo, Halibut Blanket. Front Row: William Thomas, Beaver Blanket and Bill Williams, Bear Blanket

Theophilus McBurnette: Eagle Blanket. Isabella Boyd, Cody Boyd: Raven Blankets. Katrina Boyd: Raven Blanket. Bill Williams: Bear Blanket

Alvina Martinez of the Neix. Adi Clan in cedar bark hat and Eagle Blanket.

Neix. Adi - Double Headed Eagle Button Blanket

Totem Carving

Master wood carver Nathan Jackson's Panel Eagles and pencil drawing of another project.

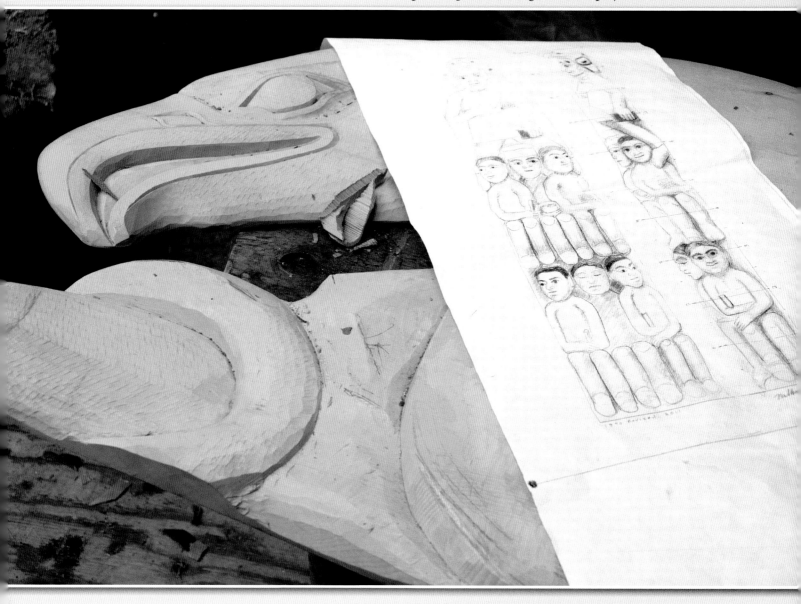

Master Tlingit carver Nathan Jackson swings an adz to carve a Family History Pole for a father and six sons for a private commission.

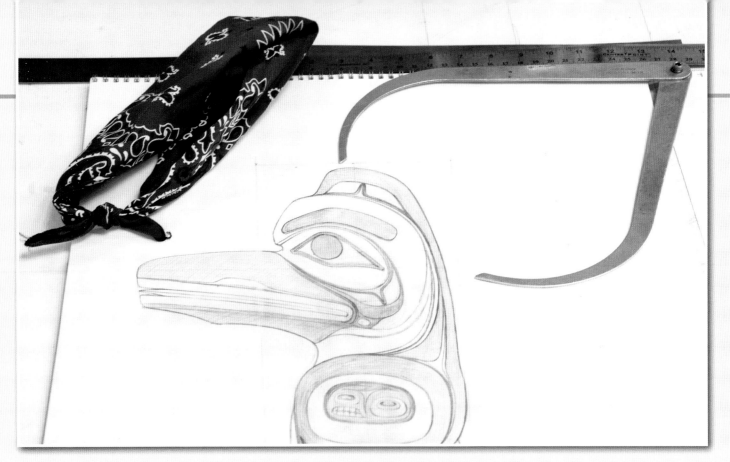

A pencil drawing by Donald Varnel beneath kerchief and calipers illustrates a classic raven head.

Nathan Jackson carves the knee of one of six sons that appear on a Family History Pole.

Master Carver Nathan Jackson takes a break from his work in the Saxman carving shed erected in 1989.

A wide array of carving and cutting tools hang nearby as Master Carver Nathan Jackson cuts into a red cedar totem pole.

Beaver House

An aging Bear Entrance Pole oversees the entry to the Beaver Clan House. The Bear represents one of the clan crests of Southeast Alaska's Tlingit Indians.

The Chief Ebbits Pole is topped by a bear. It stands in front of the William Seward Shame Pole, at right. Chief Ebbits hosted former U.S. Sec. of State William Seward when he came to Alaska in 1869, two years after purchasing Alaska from Czar Alexander II of Russia.

Raven Moon Totem in front of the Beaver Clan House.

The Beaver Clan House flanked by the Raven Pole, at left, with outspread wings and the William Seward Shame Pole, at right.

The Bear Entrance Pole – In the rain-soaked environment of Southeast Alaska, poles deteriorate quickly in the open. Although the pole carvers did not develop wood preservatives, they frequently used highly rot-resistant red cedar for their poles which lasted longer than other woods. To this day cedar is used for fence posts and exterior shakes because they resist rot from water so well.

Saxman dancer Crista Seludo emerges from the Beaver Clan House with a pair of matching Raven Totems along the entry stairway.

A Neix. Adi Memorial Pole near the corner of the Beaver Clan House displays, from top to bottom, a beaver, eagle and halibut.

A curious couple navigates Killer Whale Ave. in Saxman Totem Park

Left: Dancer Bill Williams represents a standing bear in front of the screen at the back of the Beaver Clan House.

A dancing Bill Williams in the beautiful all wood Beaver Clan House at Saxman Totem Park.

Bill Williams spreads his arms to disclose a bear at the center of his costume.

Left to Right: Tempa Major, Theophilus McBurnette, Lakrisha Hargrove, Clarita Seludo, Crista Seludo and Katrina Boyd dance in button blankets before a beautifully carved wooden screen in the Beaver Clan House.

Elder Sherrie Potter dances with Isabella Boyd, from a new generation of Tlingit dancers.

Teresa DeWitt, Joe Thomas, Tempa Major, William Thomas, Maria Badgley, Billy White, Yvonne Watson, Gabriella Daniels, Clarita Seludo, Tim Eide Jr. Bill Williams and Alvina Martinez display their beautiful costumes while chanting and dancing to the beat of the drum.

Crista Seludo,
Katrina Boyd and
Isabella Boyd dance
in button blankets
and moccasins.

Geraldine Watson, Alvina Martinez, and Joe Thomas sing and dance.

The Saanya Kwaan Cape Fox Dancers entertain visitors throughout the summer in the beautifully carved Beaver Clan House.

Elder Joe Thomas explains Tlingit traditions while standing in front of the elaborate totemic screen at the back of the Beaver Clan House.